THEN *&* NOW

LA JOLLA

OPPOSITE: Believed to be from the late 1870s, this photograph represents the earliest image of La Jolla in the La Jolla Historical Society's archival collection. It is a stereopticon view of picnickers in what is now Scripps Park, adjacent to La Jolla Cove. They have arrived with horses and carriages, most probably on an excursion from San Diego to explore this barren seaside. (Courtesy of La Jolla Historical Society.)

THEN & NOW

LA JOLLA

Carol Olten, Rudy Vaca,
and the La Jolla Historical Society

Published by Arcadia Publishing
Charleston, South Carolina

Printed in the United States of America

Then and Now is a registered trademark and is used under license from
Salamander Books Limited

For all general information, please contact Arcadia Publishing:
Telephone 843-853-2070
Fax 843-853-0044
E-mail sales@arcadiapublishing.com
For customer service and orders:
Toll-Free 1-888-313-2665

Visit us on the Internet at www.arcadiapublishing.com

On the Front Cover: La Jolla Cove has been a destination for beachgoers and picnickers since the first horses and carriages brought adventurers from San Diego to enjoy this special spot on the edge of the blue Pacific bordered by rock formations and sand stone cliffs. The earlier photograph shows a crowd enjoying the cove when a few beach cottages were all that was built along the hillsides in the early 1900s. In the later image, another crowd enjoys the cove, but the hillsides are built-up from development. (Courtesy La Jolla Historical Society.)

On the Back Cover: In 1915, Scripps Institution of Oceanography occupied a lone and barren landscape by the Pacific, far removed from the small La Jolla village beginning to take shape slightly south of it. The Biological Grade—a dirt roadway—was the only way into La Jolla from the north and was dusty in the summer and slippery in the winter, when rainstorms hit the coast. (Courtesy La Jolla Historical Society.)

CONTENTS

ACKNOWLEDGMENTS

The La Jolla Historical Society has more than 10,000 vintage photographs in its archival collection, a portion of which are reproduced in this book. The collection began with donations in the 1940s, when the first historical publication on the community, *La Jolla Year by Year*, was written by Howard S. F. Randolph. The historical society acknowledges the many donations, ranging from casual snapshots to professional photographs, that have taken place over the years. They have contributed greatly to the visual preservation of La Jolla history. Other acknowledgements are to the many board members, interns, volunteers, and docents who have contributed time, effort, and encouragement to the creation of this book—specifically Christopher King and Kathy Tran, who assisted so much as the final publication deadline approached, and Rudy Vaca, whose photographs recorded today's La Jolla. Final thanks to proofreader Ann Zahner and fellow staff members Michael Mishler and Kristina Gibbons as well as the society's executive director, John Bolthouse, whose encouraging efforts are greatly appreciated.

INTRODUCTION

When changes in urban landscape are observed on a day-to-day basis, they often slide by virtually unnoticed. An old building goes down; another replaces it. A block that once looked shabby undergoes gentrification; now it is suburban perfection.

But when changes are reviewed over a lengthy period of time, they seem monumental. In this manner, these photographs become extremely revealing, many showing La Jolla over a span of 100 years, from when the community began in 1887 to the present day of great growth and development. Streets that once were peaceful dirt pathways lined with eucalyptus now are congested, noticeably trafficked thoroughfares. Beaches that were serene places of sand and solitude, photographed with single figures gazing seaward, now have masses of humanity jockeying for a place in the sun. Barren ocean-view hillsides with a pioneer scattering of perhaps two or three homes have become built-up with estate-type houses stacked high above the Pacific like an architectural layer cake.

La Jolla—known worldwide for great natural beauty, benign coastal climate, and resort atmosphere—has grown like the proverbial Topsy, and some would argue the growth and change has been somewhat topsy-turvy. Although maintaining its own postmark and identity, the community has always operated as part of the City of San Diego, which has governed building codes. This has produced both positive and negative results.

Founded by Frank T. Botsford, La Jolla began as a barren coastal territory with no freshwater and no connecting railroad. It was a pretty, but isolated, spot to settle or to visit. Small beach cottages and bungalows were the only habitations, many first built as rentals for summer and winter visitors. The year 1896 witnessed the arrival of newspaper heiress Ellen Browning Scripps, whose vast philanthropic effort over the next 36 years of her life as a La Jollan added much to the social, cultural, and educational growth of the small Southern California beach town. The many Irving Gill–designed buildings that she encouraged and endowed remain today as the distinguishing heart of the village.

Two decades in particular—the 1920s and the 1960s—witnessed the greatest changes in La Jolla's seaside landscape. The residential development of La Jolla Shores and the Muirlands; the building of major hotels La Valencia, Casa Manana, and Colonial Inn; and the beginning of the electric railway connecting to San Diego all took place during the prosperous 1920s. In the 1960s, with the great expansion of Scripps Institution of Oceanography and the start of the University of California, San Diego (UCSD) campus and the Salk Institute, La Jolla no longer was a small internally focused village but a mecca where "town met gown" and scholars from around the world came to visit and to live. This created a new intellectual climate and café society where having a cup of coffee could lead to a chat with someone like the late and great Dr. Jonas Salk.

Throughout La Jolla's history, however, many well-known scientists, educators, artists, writers, musicians, and persons connected with the dramatic arts have called La Jolla home. Among the first was German-born Anna Held, who arrived in 1894, purchased ocean cliff property, and began the Green Dragon Colony that eventually became 12 cottages inhabited by cultural denizens from all over Europe. Much later arrivals included Theodor Geisel (Dr. Seuss), Raymond Chandler, Max Miller, Cliff Robertson, Gregory Peck, Walt Mason, and many others. Two of these, in particular, have parodied and caricatured La Jolla in their work: Dr. Seuss based many of his children's book characters on what he observed of local people and places, and Miller wrote a book called *The Town With a Funny Name,* in which he satirized the pronunciation of the town's name (the Spanish *j* like *h* instead of the English *j*) as well as the people and attitudes he found here. "We are legal," Miller wrote in 1948 noting the special La Jolla postmark, "and, I think, we also are a mood."

Many moods of La Jolla are reiterated in the oral histories recorded as part of the archives of the La Jolla Historical Society, particularly those remembering the early years of carefree living by the beach in an idyllic climate of sea breezes and sunshine where a vine-covered cottage and a garden of hollyhocks seemed to fulfill most of life's needs and demands. The moods recorded by Marnie Hutchinson of her childhood growing up during the pre–World War II summers in the historic Windemere cottage are particularly poignant. "Home was La Jolla," she wrote of her recollections here. "Hills so sweet with sage it made your head dizzy and your heart beat fast. . . . Home was the Cove where you learned to swim at four or five, a beach of rough white sand that felt grainy and clean and delicious under your bare feet . . . the village where everybody knew everybody . . . cliffs splashed with purple flowers that sang out into the sun."

The flowers, the cliffs, the village, the sand, and the sea are all still very much La Jolla. But the mood has changed from then to now. La Jolla has grown out, and La Jolla has grown up. La Jolla "Then" is a faraway place from La Jolla "Now."

CHAPTER 1

BY THE BEAUTIFUL SEA

The ocean's marine and bird life inspired countless amateur photographers in La Jolla's early history. But Leopold Hugo's arrival in 1908 exposed these subjects to professional photography for the first time. Hugo took hundreds of poetic shots of the surf and sea and here captures the graceful flight of a seagull poised in a misty sky.

La Jolla Cove has been a festive gathering place for Fourth of July celebrations since the 1890s, when thousands took the train from San Diego to swim, picnic, and watch pyrotechnic displays at the beach. This photograph shows the cove in 1924, when the community staged a special "Jollification" event on July 4 to celebrate the opening of hotels, the electric railroad, and other new amenities marking up-and-coming tourist attractions. Today the La Jolla Cove continues to draw crowds for the holiday.

An undated but timeless photograph shows two young women in billowing long dresses and high-button shoes enjoying the cove beach on a solitary day, probably back in the 1890s. One is smiling while the other tilts her head and squints toward the camera as if the sun is too bright. This is the sort of old photograph that invites a story: Are they sisters? Are they sharing a secret? A gentleman in a suit and hat inhabits the far left of the picture. What is his relation, if any? Meanwhile in the present day other stories are suggested.

Landmark rock formations, carved by the surf over thousands of years, have fascinated visitors from the very beginning. This is the legendary Alligator Head at the tip of the cove as it appeared on a postcard early in the 1900s. Pieces of it collapsed as the century progressed, primarily due to the pounding of heavy surf during winter storms. The last of the bridge to the tip of the rock (the alligator's nose) disappeared in the 1970s. This is Alligator Head as it appears today—a rock rubble and, alas, no longer an alligator.

14

The late 19th century held a fascination for the predisposition of images onto particular subject matter, the endless game of what someone sees is what the person thinks he sees and not necessarily what is there. Historically one side of Alligator Head was identified for many years as Sphinx Head Cave because of the sphinx silhouette that appeared to the naked eye. After the rock's bridge collapsed, the sphinx was no longer there—and for any such sightings tourists just had to head for the Giza Plateau. A postcard image shows the La Jolla sphinx in the early 1900s; the scene is now some rocks and water.

4607. Sphinx Head Cave, La Jolla, near San Diego, Cal.

More illusions: Queen Victoria's likeness was read into the massive Cathedral Rock that towered above the ocean sand off Coast Boulevard near the present-day Casa de Manana. In a 1905 photograph, two figures are dwarfed in the shadow of the rock as they look out to sea through the signature Queen Victoria silhouette. In fact, the rock was about 40 feet tall. But in the winter of 1906, the massive stone succumbed to high surf, and Queen Victoria was seen no more. Today the great Pacific makes its own statement.

La Jolla's magnificent Seven Caves—high vertical sandstone cliffs near Goldfish Point where the sea lapped inside the topographical formation at seven points that were sometimes reachable by foot at low tide—were an immediate tourist draw of the 1890s. The first railroad running from San Diego to La Jolla advertised visits at low tide. Here a group from that era shares the fascination of the caves' mysteries. The caves came to be celebrated in books and poetry, including in the work of *The Wonderful Wizard of Oz* author L. Frank Baum, who wrote the children's book *The Sea Fairies* based on the ocean caverns. They remain much the same tourist attraction today, although visits are more often by kayak.

Swimming and boating occupied visitors to La Jolla Cove near the beginning of the 20th century, although a few were content to keep their formal street clothes on and go for a stroll or watch the others at sport. In 1917, around the time of this postcard image, La Jolla citizens adopted a bathing suit ordinance to discourage skimpy attire at the beach and actually fine and arrest those who dared to walk in bathing clothes on the streets. The ordinance met with consternation and debate and was dropped within a year. In more contemporary times, La Jolla introduced a nude beach, but today at the cove discretion prevails.

BY THE BEAUTIFUL SEA

Although diving was yet to be a popular sport, the fascinating marine life around La Jolla Cove evoked considerable interest. In the early 1900s, a little glass bottom boat began to take visitors on rowing trips from the cove to Goldfish Point, where colorful garibaldi were a delightful sight. The boat became a fixture at the cove for many years, enjoyed by locals as well as tourists. Early La Jollans fondly recall its presence in oral histories. But as beach crowds grew, launching became difficult and the little glass bottom boat simply floated into history. Today the cove beach is for swimming and diving; no motorboats are allowed.

2936 – Bathing Beach, La Jolla, San Diego, California.

This is a group having a picnic at La Jolla Cove in 1910. Their attire demands attention. Sitting at the base of the bathhouse (upper right), they are dressed in "Sunday best" clothing. The girls have hats and fashionable dresses, and the boys wear suits and berets. (Nobody is in flip-flops or barefoot.) They are eating from picnic hampers, and the cups being raised are china, not paper or plastic. A hundred years later, a similar group has a beach picnic dressed in 2010 California casual and eating 2010 California casual. A china cup is something for collectors. A bathhouse? Who's kidding?

This old photograph was taken in March 1899 and shows the cove beach with the hillside behind dotted with a sparse collection of cottages. The farthest on the left was called the Shag. Middle to right center is the Brockton Villa, built as a private residence in 1894. At the right are a few of the 12 cottages that were built in the 1890s as part of the Green Dragon Colony. Today the Brockton Villa, restored for current use as a restaurant, is the only remaining building. The highly valued coastal property has been many times over rebuilt with larger homes and condominium residences.

Belvederes were built along La Jolla beaches in the early days to afford semi-sheltered spots to enjoy ocean views. This *c.* 1900 one at the cove had a particularly decorative touch with Gothic tracery along the roofline and board and batten siding around the skirt. There is also a handmade wooden bench sitting outside of it. Today the belvederes remain a signature of cove beaches maintained by the City of San Diego. This one is at the same site as the older one, but all hint of Gothic Revival architecture has long been lost.

Viewed from afar in the summer of 1913 and framed by eucalyptus and pine trees, La Jolla Cove was an elysian sight of endlessly blue ocean and frothy white surf. Alligator Head, the last of which was destroyed by heavy surf in the late 1970s, is a magnificent rock promontory just beyond the pine tree. A nest of Australian tea trees has just been planted near by. And the bathhouse, to be torn down in 1924, is a major focus to the left. What remains of this sight nearly 100 years later are the gnarled tea trees and the timeless ocean and surf kissed by the sun and capped by the sky.

Ocean beaches as a place to enjoy healthful fresh air and amusements was a growing phenomenon of the mid- to late 19th century, particularly in France and England. In the United States, it spread with the opening of Coney Island and inevitably moved to the West Coast, where the Pacific's expansive beaches offered more than enough room for frolic and amusement. La Jolla Cove's bathhouse became a popular gathering place as the 20th century dawned and, for a brief time, large swings were erected for bodies to oscillate with the ocean breezes.

In 1902, a German entrepreneur named Prof. Gustav Schulz began to dig a tunnel from the cliff into one of the ocean caves with the idea of charging visitors a few cents for the descent to the bottom via a rope. He was successful, and the cave's reputation grew in time to be named Sunny Jim, after a cartoon character. The cave continues as a tourist attraction today although the trip down is made by stairs, not rope. It is operated as part of the Cave Store at 1325 Cave Street in La Jolla, owned by Jim Allen.

This line of palm trees has been a La Jolla icon since it was first planted in the early 1900s by La Jolla pioneer Walter Lieber, himself transplanted from a wealthy family in Philadelphia. The palms are a familiar and much-photographed signature along the Coast Boulevard side of Scripps Park. This postcard image of them is from the 1940s, when they were allowed to develop long beards from drooping dead fronds. The dead fronds are now cut off seasonally, giving the trees fresh haircuts. New trees have been interplanted recently so that as the old ones die La Jolla will have palms for posterity. The life of a palm tree is estimated at 100 years.

CHAPTER 2

HOME SWEET HOME

Green Dragon Colony founder Anna Held built her beloved Wahnfried home high on a La Jolla cliff in 1894, starting by first putting up the fireplace. She filled the interior with many handmade items, and the residence soon became a cozy gathering place for well-known artists from around the world, lending much to La Jolla's reputation.

The first permanent home in La Jolla was built in 1887 at the corner of Silverado Street and Exchange Place by George Heald, a pioneer who had invested in his lot in an auction held the same year. Built in the Victorian Stick style with chinoiserie details on the front porch, the house took advantage of ocean views toward Goldfish Point and La Jolla Cove. Heald's corner now has a contemporary wood-and-glass home enveloped by pine trees and bamboo, but the old "farm" home cistern remains intact nearby.

Florence Palmer epitomized the internationally travelled and cultured person who came to La Jolla to live in the early 1900s. In 1905, she built this home for herself at 1428 Soledad Avenue and named it Thandara, or House of Dreams. The architecture combined ideas of Japanese design with California craftsman style. Extensive gardens also were planted and developed in the Japanese style with more than 300 exotic trees. Today the home remains in private ownership and is surrounded by dense, mature landscape.

This house is typical of the vine-covered cottages first built in La Jolla in the 1890s—except it is two-stories instead of one and more Victorian in style than the common craftsman bungalows. Olivia Mudgett built it as a private residence named the Villa Waldo on Girard Avenue, when the street had more residential and less of the present-day commercial development. As Girard developed as a business area, the house was moved to a back lot on Drury Lane where it continues to be used today as rental property—an anachronism in the midst of village commercial life.

When first built in the mid-1890s, the Brockton Villa stood against a sparse hillside with spectacular views of the North Shore and La Jolla Cove. A doctor from San Diego planned it as a beach retreat, but he died in an accident in 1896, and the house was left as rental property for many years. In the early 1990s, Pannikin coffeehouse owner Bob Sinclair pursued the idea of creating a restaurant in the old home. It thrives today as a popular La Jolla eatery with the best view in town.

The Red Roost and Red Rest cottages on Coast Boulevard across from La Jolla's landmark Scripps Park have been, as of 2010, slowly falling into ruin for more than four decades—despite continuing preservation efforts to save them as landmark buildings reflecting the California bungalow architecture of the 1890s. Community preservationists committed both cottages to the national and city register of historic properties in the mid-1970s after the owner had planned to tear them down and build a new hotel on the oceanfront site. They were not torn down. But today they remain in decay.

The Bowman family of La Jolla was justly proud of this small two-story wood-siding house they built after moving west from Illinois in the early 1900s. They put it on a picture postcard with Alfred Bowman shown on a horse out front in 1909 at 601 Marine Street. Alfred mailed the postcard to his brother Martin Allen Bowman, who had remained in Illinois, with a note seeming to evoke envy: "I send you a picture of our home in Cala. And myself as a tough cowpuncher. Best regards from us all. Alfred." The newer image shows the property as it appears today.

Small houses played a lot of musical chairs in the early days of La Jolla, moving from lot to lot and street to street as the commercial and residential areas were constantly reconfiguring. This house, a fine example of the California craftsman bungalow built by the Victor Wier family, originally stood at 7855 Fay Avenue at the start of the 1900s. When the site was purchased in mid-century for a bowling alley, it was moved to the corner of Marine Street and La Jolla Boulevard. Finally it came to rest at 525 Marine Street before it was demolished.

La Jolla's first historian, Howard Randolph, who wrote the initial history of the village called *La Jolla Year by Year*, lived here at 7944 Prospect Place in the 1930s and early 1940s. The address was part of a little extension of Prospect beyond the commercial zone across Torrey Pines Road, noted for its closeness to the village, great north shore views, and seclusion from traffic. The neighborhood remains intact today as a residential zone prized for its proximity to the village.

H. Austin Adams, who built this house on the Park Row circle in 1908, named it The Dreamery. He was a playwright from New York and had a little tower designed as part of the house as a place where he could "dream" and be inspired to write more plays. But when he put it up for sale he advertised it with a closet full of rejected manuscripts and two built-in mortgages. That was about 100 years ago. Author Carol Olten has the good fortune to own this house today—with one mortgage—and that same closet is filled with clothes and not rejected manuscripts.

The illustrious architect Irving Gill designed this house in the early 1900s, now part of the Scripps-Gill cultural zone in the village and restored in an adaptive reuse as the Bed and Breakfast Inn of La Jolla. It features tilt-up concrete construction similar to the nearby La Jolla Woman's Club and the La Jolla Recreation Center. For many years, the house was home to the family of "March King" John Philip Sousa and was covered with vines as seen in the older photograph. As a bed and breakfast, the house is noted for its old-fashioned gardens, where tea and breakfast is often served.

Built in 1904 and known as Wisteria Cottage for the vine-covered pergola that cascades with purple blossoms each spring, this house is now owned by the La Jolla Historical Society and used primarily for rotating exhibits having to do with La Jolla history. It was purchased by Eliza Virginia Scripps shortly after it was built and was owned by Scripps family descendants before the late Ellen Revelle and her four children donated it to the historical society in July 2008 along with two other historic structures adjacent, now used as an office and archival storage.

The nationally known literary scribe Walt Mason had this modest bungalow at 1411 Virginia Way as his California residence after moving here from Emporia, Kansas. A short, stout man who walked La Jolla streets with a red cocker spaniel, Mason was a familiar figure here, often found sitting in village coffee shops and soda fountains writing his rhyming riddles, syndicated in the nation's newspapers. The house on Virginia Way now has historic designation and appears much as when Mason lived there—minus, of course, the little push mower on the front lawn.

Ellen Browning Scripps built the first residence in La Jolla on a genuinely grand scale in 1896—a Victorian mansion with a tower and conservatory rooms overlooking the ocean. Hillsides terraced to the sea were planted with colorful flowers on the back, or ocean side, of the property. Scripps was a great believer in beauty of all sorts and keeping La Jolla "in harmony with its glorious natural setting" as she declared in 1913. Today the ocean side of her property is now the sculpture garden of the Museum of Contemporary Art, with some signature plantings still remaining intact from Scripps's period.

3866—Scripps Residence, La Jolla, San Diego, California.

When Ellen Browning Scripps's first home burned in an arsonist fire in 1915, she promptly set to work to build a second residence on the same site designed in a modern Cubist style by architect Irving Gill, whom she was working with on many cultural and civic buildings in La Jolla. The house again was named South Moulton Villa and had a wide, arched entrance as seen from its Prospect Street side. Upon her death here in 1932, the house remained vacant for nine years until it became the Art Center. Today the site is the location for the Museum of Contemporary Art.

Philip Barber, an investor from New Jersey, purchased extensive property along the sand dunes south of the village in 1921 and hired architect Herbert Palmer to design an expansive Mediterranean-style home for his family. The Barber family lived in the residence for many years, and the land around it was gradually sold off in individual lots that became La Jolla's residential area known as the Barber Tract. The actor Cliff Robertson, a La Jolla native, purchased the Barber home at 325 Dunemere Lane and used it as a primary and secondary residence over the years. Today the house and grounds remain one of the prime pieces of Southern California real estate.

Harold James Muir had an elysian dream for "that beautiful land with sweeping view of sea and hill" known as La Jolla's Muirlands. Coming here with investment money from Colorado in the mid-1920s, he purchased 257 acres overlooking the ocean with plans to develop large estates beginning with his own—a Spanish-style residence designed by architect Edgar Ullrich surrounded by orchards and flora. Muir's dream for grand estates fizzled with the arrival of the Great Depression, but his own home remains one of La Jolla's finest and largest, often referred to as "the Versailles of La Jolla."

Coast Boulevard and Coast Boulevard South were lined with small, single-story cottages basically until the 1960s, when the condominium phenomenon began to considerably alter the landscape. The first and tallest, built over much controversy, was the landmark tower completed in 1963 at 939 Coast Boulevard, which vastly changed the small scale quality of the village. Coastal height limitations curtailed more high-rises after that, but condos within the new 30-foot limit continued to replace single-family dwellings. Today the oceanside lots are virtually built-up with condominium developments in multiple architectural styles.

CHAPTER 3

MAIN STREET STUDIES

Street beautification has been an important issue in La Jolla since the earliest days. An old wooden watering trough for horses once stood at the corner of Girard Avenue and Prospect Street in the early 1900s, but it was replaced in 1909 by an ornamental stone and wood structure that soon became a picturesque landmark covered with bougainvillea.

It is hard to imagine today, but La Jolla's main commercial artery—Girard Avenue—once was a romantic-looking landscape of small cottages shaded by eucalyptus trees. This view shows an unpaved street with the small house at right that housed the post office. Today's scene is of many varied storefronts with the right of the photograph showing the large Union Bank building and the street filled with lines of stores.

This large commercial building was built at 7824 Girard Avenue in 1919. At street level, it housed the Barnes and Calloway grocery and the La Jolla Post Office. The upstairs was a meeting room for the La Jolla Brotherhood men's organization. Next-door on the left was the home and office of Dr. Martha Dunn Corey, a much-loved and respected physician. Corey's modest house was moved many years ago, but the large commercial building remains in use as the well-known Burns Drugs.

An important corner was established at Wall Street and Girard Avenue when this building went up in 1924, and the Granada Theater—the one and only of La Jolla's ornate movie palaces—opened as one of two major lessees. Ironically the other was the United States National Bank. La Jollans enjoyed many silent picture shows at the Granada, and the first talkie came in 1929—Mary Pickford in *Coquette*. When the Granada closed in 1952, the building became a department store before it was torn down in the 1980s to make room for this larger complex.

The Cove Theater opened in 1952 at 7730 Girard Avenue and quickly became a much-loved and popular motion picture house managed by the venerated Spencer Wilson. It remained so until closing some 50 years later, leaving many La Jollans teary-eyed. Progress brought two new businesses on Girard—a men's clothing store and a French furniture venture that are in operation at the spot today, but movie fans seldom pass by without remembering that one endless summer when the Cove offered an entire three months of *Cinema Paradiso*.

The 1940s witnessed many changes along Girard Avenue and Wall Street, especially after the end of World War II, when the community could forget the worries of a Japanese attack along the coastline and return to the serious business of shopping. Iller's department store, at right, became an established landmark around the corner from the old Granada Theater and across the street from the Athenaeum Art and Music Library, a private membership organization now remaining but at that time leased to the City of San Diego for operation of the La Jolla Public Library.

This streetscape shows the west side of Girard Avenue as it appeared in the late 1950s with several anchor stores featuring mid-century modern facades that represented the "bones" of the business community. Today two of them—Warwick's bookstore and Burns Drugs—are still mainstays of the community. But Burriston's shoes, Frazee's paint, and John's market are long out of business and have been replaced by varieties of tenants over the past five decades.

Pictured in the late 1950s, this busy intersection of Girard Avenue and Silverado Street shows one of La Jolla's lost architectural treasures—the First National Bank building at left designed by architect Richard Requa. It was erected in 1929 and contained a large mural painted by the artist Hugo Ballin. The structure was demolished in 1972 to make room for today's Union Bank building, but the mural was resurrected at the La Jolla Recreation Center where it remains today. The same era witnessed the disappearance of the car business on the other corner and construction of the present bank building.

Quon Mane, a store specializing in carved teak furniture, hand-printed Japanese screens, antique porcelain, and many unusual gift items of Asian derivation, typified the often unique shopping opportunities La Jolla offered in mid-century before national and international chains moved onto Girard Avenue. It was located at 7848 Girard and noted for its quaint two-story building with chinoiserie front ornamentation. The building remains today as a rug store, but the facade and shopping opportunities are quite different.

The Southern Trust and Savings Bank opened in this new building at Girard Avenue and Prospect Street in 1916 featuring a party with an orchestra and fruit punch. It gave another large party about a decade later when the bank remodeled but kept the building's rounded facade built to fit the corner. After the bank closed, the Rexall Drugstore chain took over the location, again remodeling but keeping the curve of the corner. Today a rug store occupies the building, whose curves remain evident.

This is a postcard view of La Valencia hotel looking up from the ocean side at Scripps Park. The hotel was built in 1926, and its iconic tower was added two years later. Today the hotel and its tile-domed tower remain significant landmarks, although condominium developments along Coast Boulevard have altered the immediate landscape. The hotel also changed its own landscape in the 1990s when it added considerably to its suite rentals by building down the hillside.

This is the northern entrance to La Jolla on Prospect Street from Torrey Pines Road as it appeared on a *c.* 1910 postcard. Prospect is not yet paved, and part of the Green Dragon Colony appears on the right. The rail and concrete retaining wall erected to keep automobiles and people from sliding down onto Cave Street, which leads to the cove, remain in place today. The big changes are seen along Prospect Street—restaurants, art galleries, and boutiques all built bigger and taller to take advantage of ocean views.

This is a picture postcard showing the Colonial Hotel and Little Hotel by the Sea as they appeared in the late 1920s from near the foot of Jenner Street. The first part of the Colonial was a design by architect Richard Requa constructed on Prospect Street. When the Colonial expanded in 1928, that building was moved to Jenner and still remains in use. In 1925, a smaller hotel was built by a different owner on Jenner, at the intersection with South Coast Boulevard. Today the Grande Colonial La Jolla owns and operates the entire property.

When La Jolla founding father Frank Botsford was developing La Jolla Park in the late 1880s, one of his enticements to buyers was the planting of 2,000 trees on the barren, desert-like landscape. Besides signature palms, they included many eucalyptus planted along Herschel Avenue, looking toward the ocean with the Cabrillo Hotel, constructed in 1908, in the background along with the infamous little Red Devil train at its stop in front. Today the Cabrillo remains (operated as part of La Valencia), and the train is long gone. But a token eucalyptus still stands.

CHAPTER

4

MIND AND MATTER

Thanks primarily to the philanthropy of the Scripps family, La Jolla was endowed with outstanding educational, cultural, medical, scientific, religious, and social institutions early in its history. Many of the buildings housing these institutions were the result of donations from Ellen Browning Scripps and her half-sister Eliza Virginia working with the exceptional architect Irving Gill. Much of the legacy remains intact today.

Designed by architect Irving Gill, the La Jolla Woman's Club features graceful arches and columns and the architect's signature tilt-up concrete construction. The *c.* 1925 photograph shows it about a decade after it was built and the landscape had begun to mature. In its early years, the club's main hall was used for theatrical presentations; La Jolla's first productions of Shakespeare's plays were staged here. Today the building continues to be privately owned by the woman's club and is often rented for weddings and receptions.

The La Jolla Sanitarium, right, was built in 1918 and had a capacity of only 20 beds. As La Jolla's population grew, Ellen Browning Scripps donated funds for a new hospital, completed in 1924 with a capacity for 56 beds. Known as Scripps Hospital, the landmark medical facility continued in operation into the 1960s, when need for expansion led administrators to construct new facilities outside of the immediate village. The old hospital now has been converted into exclusive condominiums, and the sanitarium is a privately owned, multiuse building.

Originally known as the Community House, the La Jolla Recreation Center was completed in 1915 and dedicated to the children of San Diego by Ellen Browning Scripps, who provided the land as well as the funding for the building, another tilt-up concrete design by Irving Gill. Generations of children have grown up using the playground around it, and the interiors continue to be used for community meetings. The grounds and building are operated under jurisdiction of the City of San Diego, which received the deed from Scripps in 1915.

The first buildings for The Bishop's School were designed by Irving Gill, erected in 1909, and include a square tower dominating the quad. The square structure was replaced by a rounded one designed by architect Carleton Winslow in 1930 that remains the signature of the exclusive private school today. Bishop's first opened as a school for girls funded by the Scripps half-sisters, who firmly believed in education as a way to humane and social improvements. Today Bishop's thrives as a high and junior high school for boys and girls known for an outstanding educational program on a beautiful campus.

The charming little Reading Room was built as a library and literary gathering place for La Jollans in the late 1890s at the corner of Girard Avenue and Wall Street—a gift to the community from a visitor named Florence Sawyer who also saw to its first furnishings and books. It remained there until a new library was built at the site in 1921, and the small Victorian structure was moved to Draper Avenue for residential use. Now it has found a final resting place on the campus of The Bishop's School, where it is used for meetings and special receptions.

This Spanish Revival–style building was designed by William Templeton Johnson with tall arched windows and classical columns at the front portico. The photograph shows it in 1921, shortly after it was completed at Girard Avenue and Wall Street for the La Jolla Library Association. In 1955, the City of San Diego took a long-term lease on the building for operation as the La Jolla Library. The library association, meanwhile, donated much of its collection to the city but retained art and music books to operate as the Athenaeum Music and Arts Library. Today it continues as a private membership library, and the La Jolla Public Library is located at a newer facility at 7555 Draper Avenue.

BEACH CLUB
LA JOLLA, CALIF.

The La Jolla Beach and Tennis Club opened in July 1927 as the La Jolla Beach and Yacht Club with plans for a harbor and breakwater to accommodate yachts travelling through a 150-foot-wide channel to the ocean. But both the harbor and breakwater had to be abandoned, most probably because of the existing presence of a submarine canyon. Designed by Hollywood architect Robert Stacey-Judd, the club buildings were in the Spanish Mediterranean style with Mayan influences. The facility became the La Jolla Beach and Tennis Club in 1935 and remains an exclusive organization today.

In the early 1920s, the committee founding the La Jolla Country Club noted people "come here to be entertained and the one form of entertainment which they demand above all others is golf." An 18-hole course was laid out and, in 1926, a proposal was made for the first clubhouse, designed by architect Herbert Mann and completed and dedicated a year later. Today, after many new buildings were added, the country club is one of the most prestigious organizations in the community.

Architect William Templeton Johnson designed the first buildings of La Jolla High School, which opened with junior-senior levels in September 1922. This photograph shows the main building of the high school as it appeared in its handsome campus setting in the 1940s. The old high school buildings were demolished in the 1970s, when they were found to not meet earthquake standards, and a new campus was created on the Nautilus Street site. It continues to serve a growing population of students today.

Elementary schools for La Jolla children were located in a variety of buildings, starting in the 1890s when the first school was held in a private home and later on the second floor of a general store. The present La Jolla Elementary School on upper Girard Avenue opened in a large educational building constructed in 1914. Early additions to the campus were made in 1926 and 1929. Continuing expansions in later years have created a much larger school, noted for its high-ranking educational programs.

The first marine scientists for the Scripps Institution of Oceanography pursued their studies from a small building at La Jolla Cove. But they soon found this location too overrun by tourists and located new facilities farther north beyond La Jolla Shores. The famous 1,000-foot pier was dedicated in 1916. This shows the pier and cluster of buildings at Scripps Oceanography in 1926. The institution became known around the world early on, but its true world-renowned fame took shape after World War II. Today's expanded campus speaks for itself.

The uniquely shaped central university library drew much attention when it opened in an eucalyptus grove on the UCSD campus in the late 1960s. The campus itself was new at the time, a product of the earlier 1960s when the university was designed to feature three clusters with four colleges within each, all widely spaced in the eucalyptus groves overlooking the Pacific. Today buildings and parking structures have replaced many of the groves and open spaces. The library, while once a towering, unique structure, appears much smaller by a 21st-century scale.

When Dr. Jonas Salk commissioned architect Louis Kahn to design the Salk Institute for Biological Studies, he asked for "a facility worthy of a visit by Pablo Picasso." Completed in 1965, the mirror-image laboratory buildings that flanked a sweeping courtyard overlooking the Pacific quickly inspired awe in the worlds of science and architecture. The institute was built just 10 years after Salk became internationally famous for his polio vaccine. An east addition was added to the facility in 1995, and plans continue for further expansion as scientists and architects from around the world continue their pilgrimages to the bold site on a cliff above the Pacific.

The La Jolla Post Office was constructed on Wall Street and dedicated in 1935 as a Works Progress Administration (WPA) project. The post office had been located in a variety of houses and storefronts before that time and after the postmark had been designated in the 1890s shortly after La Jolla was founded. For a short time, the name appeared as "Lajollee" because the *a* in the spelling was misread by the Post Office Department in Washington, D.C. Today the building appears with an annex added in the late 1950s.

St. James By-the-Sea Episcopal Church was originally built in the early 1900s in the then popular Spanish Mission Revival style of architecture. As the small church grew, this structure was moved out of the village area and reopened as the La Jolla Baptist Church at a new location. The St. James congregation then built a larger church on the original site that eventually included a tower and belfry dedicated to Eliza Virginia Scripps after her death in 1921. At present, the church remains an architectural focal point in the La Jolla cultural zone.

Casa de Manana opened as a grand, oceanfront resort hotel in 1924 and is depicted in a postcard image from that era. Attracting many famous guests, it was a setting for glamorous social soirees through the 1920s and 1930s and was noted for its Mediterranean-style architecture after a design by Edgar Ullrich. Through its early history it was fashionably attended by owner Isabel Hopkins. After she sold the facility, the glamorous scene declined. Now it is run under the same name as a high-end facility for retirement living.

The first Mary Star of the Sea Catholic Church was a small Gothic-inspired building constructed at the corner of Girard Avenue and Kline Street by a local carpenter in 1908. Designed by architect Carleton Winslow with defined arches and a signature bell tower, the present Spanish Mission–style structure replaced this church in 1935. A figurative mural with religious motifs painted by artists Alfredo Ramos Martinez decorates the entrance.

First built in 1909, this cottage was threatened with demolition to make room for a Coast Boulevard condominium. But it was rescued and moved to 7846 Eads Avenue as a home for the La Jolla Historical Society in 1981. The society continues to use it as office space today and also uses adjacent buildings—Wisteria Cottage and a carriage house—for exhibits and archival storage after a generous donation of the buildings by the Ellen and Roger Revelle family.

At one time, trains were the primary connection between San Diego and La Jolla, running along sandy beaches with scarcely a building in sight. Ironically a one-way ride took about half an hour, similar to what automobiles now take on a good traffic day. This San Carlos substation was built in 1926 at 6063 La Jolla Boulevard to accommodate passengers; it remained there until the last run in 1940. The La Jolla United Methodist Church acquired the site in 1953 and incorporated the station into new religious facilities.

MIND AND MATTER

CHAPTER

CHANGING
LANDSCAPES

This idyllic view of La Jolla depicted from above La Jolla Shores shows the coastline and small village as it appeared in the early 1920s. It was a popular spot from which to view the shoreline, and someone has taken the time to place a rustic bench on which to sit and enjoy the view. The plein air artist Alfred Mitchell painted one of his well-known canvasses from this viewpoint at about that same time. Today's scene depicts a far different scene with the 939 Coast Boulevard high-rise anchoring the point.

Looking north from just above La Jolla Shores, the Scripps Institution of Oceanography and its iconic pier are the lone marks on the landscape at right center, with a few houses in the foreground in the early 20th century. The road connecting La Jolla to Scripps, then called the Biological Grade, is unpaved and notorious for being muddy and hardly drivable after winter rains. Now highly trafficked, the street has become La Jolla Shores Drive and the area crowded with houses and condos.

South Moulton Villa, Ellen Browning Scripps's private residence from 1896 to 1932, was known for its surrounding lovely gardens tended daily by up to nine gardeners. This view, looking south toward The Bishop's School when it still had a square tower, before the rounded dome was built in 1930, dates to about 1910. It most probably was taken from Scripps's upstairs window. Today the Museum of Contemporary Art occupies the site that was her house and the In Eden apartment building has long replaced the garden.

Bird's Eye View, La Jolla, Calif.

Dirt roads and pathways connect sparse residences in this *c.* 1915 bird's-eye view of La Jolla. Prospect Street, unpaved, leads into town from Torrey Pines Road with Goldfish Point at the far right. The few cottages that formed Anna Held's Green Dragon Colony lie beyond. But the village is beginning to fill with clusters of houses. Viewed today from the same spot, the scene shows cars, traffic, commercial buildings, and an assortment of houses filling the once peaceful site where crashing waves were once the major sounds.

CHANGING LANDSCAPES

This is a *c.* 1920 view of Scripps Park looking north toward the cove and the cliffs far beyond. What remains today, of course, are the wonderful park itself and quite a lot of the original landscape. The tree at far left in the older photograph has changed shape but is still standing along with some of the low-slung Australian tea (also known as salt box) trees and the landmark line of palms. Today they are maintained without their "beards," and a generous private donation of new palms has been made to insure the linear Southern California landmark.

A train to and from San Diego once clattered along these tracks on Prospect Street. The postcard image shows the corner of Cuvier Street and Prospect in 1916 shortly after the La Jolla Recreation Center was built. Originally called the La Jolla Community House and Playground, the recreation center is in the background, and outdoor electrical lighting (progressive for the time) has already been installed. The train tracks have long disappeared, and the present scene shows the grounds of the rec center intact and very much in use.

CHANGING LANDSCAPES

a Jolla. Calif.

This mission-style terminal building was constructed in 1925 at the corner of Prospect Street and Fay Avenue to serve the electric railway that operated between La Jolla and San Diego from that time to 1940. The wire connections are visible in the picture along with one of the little cars, at far left. The building was demolished when rail service ended. The interim has witnessed several different buildings on the site, the latest being the one that formerly housed the Hard Rock Café and now is home to another restaurant.

Changing Landscapes

C. G. Rannells, operator of a livery service known as La Jolla Transfer, is at the ready with his handsome horses and wagon for transport along Prospect Street in this *c.* 1915 image showing 1270 Prospect. Anna Held's house is in the background, the main anchor of the internationally known Green Dragon Colony that she founded for artists, musicians, and the literary set in the 1890s. Today it is a construction site as a new restaurant facility is being built where the old Chart House once stood. All that remains of Held's home is a chimney, which is to be preserved in the new building.

Tooling along Prospect in an open car in 1910, a driver would have been stirring up dust from the unpaved road and enjoying a great ocean view. The only large building on the street was the Cabrillo Hotel, just built in 1908 and marketing its "light with electricity" with a large sign on top of the building. The Cabrillo remains today, operated as part of the La Valencia, itself built much later in the mid-1920s. The street is still very recognizable in the newer photograph, although many more structures housing restaurants, galleries, and shops make up the mix of businesses with ocean views.

This shows the rock retaining wall being built along Coast Boulevard on the ocean side of Ellen Browning Scripps's house around 1910. It was 400 feet long and 21 feet high at the tallest point. Fifty holes were placed in the wall, each 8 feet apart, for lights that remained until the start of World War II, when they were turned off and removed because of the blackout. Later most of the holes were filled in. The wall remains today behind the Museum of Contemporary Art, built on the site of the Scripps' house. It is sometimes used as a training place for rock climbers.

Motor Car and Hotel Cabrillo at La Jolla, San Diego, Cal.

The Cabrillo Hotel, designed by architect Irving Gill, was constructed on Prospect Street in 1908 and was for many years the only large building there. It was a popular spot for passengers to load and unload on the train or into one of the few automobiles that occupied the village in the early 20th century. The Cabrillo remains as a hotel today, run as an annex to La Valencia, which purchased the building in the late 1950s and refurbished it considerably.

CHANGING LANDSCAPES

Bird Rock Avenue was a tiny dirt road leading toward the sign on the hill advertising the community for potential development in the early 20th century. There also was a hand-built stairway going up to the sign along with a 1-mile marker used by U.S. Navy ships at sea to indicate their location. The sign disappeared over time as the community was developed into the thriving commercial and residential area that it is today. Now Bird Rock Avenue serves as an artery to the increased residential development around it.

The railroad built the Devil's Slide stairway as an access to Emerald Cove and the caves near Goldfish Point in 1899 as an enticement for visitors to come to La Jolla and explore the tide pools and beaches. The long wooden staircase descended down steep cliffs from Prospect Street and soon became a popular way to reach the shoreline to collect abalone. It eventually deteriorated, and a bridge was built over the chasm to become part of a nature trail along Goldfish Point. The beach access no longer exists.

The La Jolla Riding Academy is shown in a postcard image shortly after it was laid out in the Shores area in 1931. It was designed by architect Herbert Mann and consisted of a practice ring and another one for show. A two-story clubhouse contained 30 box stalls on the lower level, with club rooms and locker rooms upstairs. In 1948, the facility became the Rancho del Charro, and a motor hotel was added to the operation, attracting legendary figures from around the country. Today a high-rise hotel and restaurant occupies much of the old site.

CHANGING LANDSCAPES

This *c.* 1930 postcard image shows Camino de la Costa leading into the Bird Rock area. The only structure evident is the Bird Rock Inn on the ocean side point where Charles Lindbergh is said to have dined shortly before he left on his famous transatlantic flight in 1927. Most of Bird Rock's development did not happen until after World War II, when many small ranch houses were built by returning military families. Today the area is built-up to near capacity as large homes and condos take advantage of the sites' views.

9785 Moulton Villa, La Jolla, Cal.

The Ellen Browning Scripps residence with a Queen Anne–style turret stood out on Prospect Street when it originally was built in 1896 as the grandest and largest residence in La Jolla. It burned to the ground in an arsonist fire in 1915, after which Scripps built a new home at the same site, a much more modern residence designed by architect Irving Gill. Today the Prospect Street location is the home of the Museum of Contemporary Art.

The Children's Pool with its protective breakfront for swimming was a landmark engineering accomplishment when it was completed in 1932, altering the coastline of La Jolla. For many years, children learned to swim within the protective wall, and the sandy beach was a popular spot for sunbathers. Today the Children's Pool is noted for the seal population it attracts. It is also the subject of continuing controversy over whether the area should be used by seals or people.

DISCOVER THOUSANDS OF LOCAL HISTORY BOOKS FEATURING MILLIONS OF VINTAGE IMAGES

Arcadia Publishing, the leading local history publisher in the United States, is committed to making history accessible and meaningful through publishing books that celebrate and preserve the heritage of America's people and places.

Find more books like this at
www.arcadiapublishing.com

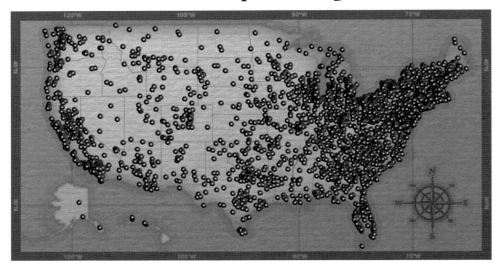

Search for your hometown history, your old stomping grounds, and even your favorite sports team.

MADE IN THE USA